dentsu social media handbook

Grow outward. Grow inward.

Popular Prakashan
www.popularprakashan.com

Popular Prakashan Pvt. Ltd.
301, Mahalaxmi Chambers
22, Bhulabhai Desai Road
Mumbai 400026

ISBN 978-81-7991-605-6
(4353)

Disclaimer:
Dentsu Marcom India Pvt Ltd and the publishers make no representations or warranties with respect to any information contained in this book and shall not be responsible or liable for any errors, inaccuracies or omissions in relation to the information contained herein. We acknowledge and thank all the sources on the worldwide web that we have drawn upon for the information in this book. However, neither the publishers nor Dentsu Marcom India Ltd take responsibility for the same.

Printed by
Lustra Print

Published by
Ramdas Bhatkal for
Popular Prakashan Pvt. Ltd.
301, Mahalaxmi Chambers
22, Bhulabhai Desai Road
Mumbai 400026

This handbook is the combined effort of

Sanjay Kumar
Dilipkarthik J
Parul Rangnekar Singh
Sourav Dutta
Nupur Maskara
Snigdha Nandan
Rakesh Chhaunkar
Shahid Hussain
Jeetander Singh
Nimisha Sharma
Samrat Sinha
Najum-U-Saquib Lachoo
Rajendra Kumar
Gaurav Tandon
Molly Monga
Sudheer Varanasi
Tirtha Bose
Dushyant Chopra
S.M. Salim
Beduin Roy
Shivram Choudhary
Naresh Gupta

Our special thanks to

Rahul Saighal
Basant Dhawan
Himanshu Bharadwaj
Neville Braganza
Rajesh Aggarwal
Ramesh Thakur
Krishna Prasad

And everyone else at Aircel and Dentsu who were directly or indirectly involved in the creation of this handbook.

Aircel Academy

People are the greatest resource of any organisation. At Aircel we believe that they have made Aircel what it is today. And it is only when people are nurtured, that sustained growth can be achieved by any organisation.

This is why the Aircel Academy came into being. To maximise the growth potential of every Aircelite, to ensure that the growth is holistic, encompassing both individual development and enhanced contribution to the organisation. The Academy aims to create leaders who will look at the future, and not the past, who will constantly create new solutions to meet ever-new challenges.

The Aircel Academy, located in the business hub of Gurgaon, is a sprawling 25,000 sq. ft campus, equipped with state-of-the-art learning tools. Our faculty has excellent teachers from within and outside the organisation, who will impart the best training possible in the field of technology, sales, service management, professional support services and general management.

With cutting-edge virtual classrooms and offsite training modules, the Aircel Academy is designed to reach every single Aircelite, no matter where he or she is located.

We invite you to explore the Aircel Academy.

Foreword

Some years ago, the very suggestion that sociology, anthropology and psychology could one day seamlessly intersect technology, would have seemed preposterous. Today the marriage of all these is social media.

We know from our daily experience that consumers don't always believe what you tell them. They may also only rarely believe what you show them. Thankfully, they often believe what their friends tell them. But most importantly, they always believe what they tell themselves. That is really the essence of the emergence of social media, as we know it today. The consumer is at the centre of the new universe : his universe.

As an innovator-pioneer brand, we at Aircel have always believed in not only embracing change, but also leading it. However, this requires the constant curiosity of a child, and the dedication of a pupil, before you can imbibe new ideas or mould yourself to respond to new stimuli. The ignition of social media forces is fairly recent. It requires understanding and appreciation.

Our sponsorship of the Dentsu Social Media Handbook is a first step in that direction.

Gurdeep Singh,
COO,
Aircel

Preface

At McDonald's, the fast-food chain, the simple belief is, "Our head of social media is the customer."

Nothing could be more appropriate in today's digitally-charged marketplace. In most organizations, social media is still part jargon, part buzz-word. It is not a customer-centric marketing approach, but just a necessary sub-part of every brand-manager's standard presentation, lest he or she be labelled old-fashioned. Few marketers, unfortunately, understand that social media are about the 4 new 'E's of brand health : empathy, enthusiasm, engagement and endearment. Well used, social media can produce seismographic impact.

In all traditional media, the accent has always been on 'pay' as a pre-condition to succeed with communication. The more money that irrigates the campaign, the farther your message will go. In social media, the key to success is not 'pay', but 'play' ... your brand has to have the ability to engage with consumers, converse with them, listen to them, respond to them, get to know them, address their concerns ... money matters, but only marginally.

We at Dentsu Digital are proud to put out this handbook. It is meant to be a ready primer for those who are new to social media ... to be honest, most of us are ... and that is nothing to be ashamed of. Every one of us starts as a beginner. Learning new jargon, imbibing new trends and understanding change is part of every marketer's journey closer to the consumer's heart. We hope this compilation by the Dentsu team helps do just that for you.

Sandeep Goyal,
Chairman,
Dentsu India

Table of Contents

1 Introduction

Where is the market place now?

In yesterday's market place, brands spoke to consumers and consumers did what the brands asked them to do. It was an age in which brands didn't engage in a dialogue with consumers. The brands controlled the conversation and the way the image of the brand was built.

Today the market place is about brands and consumers speaking to each other. Brands have been losing control over the kind of conversation that is taking place about the brand. The Internet has moved the control of brands into consumers' hands, and that is posing new challenges for brand owners. What it means is that today, brand owners either need to have more people speaking positively about the brands or have fewer people speaking negatively. In both cases Social Media play a crucial role.

Social Media provide a hangout for people where they informally and anonymously, if they so wish, share everything about their lives. They talk about their tastes and preferences for various products, they rave, they rant, they divulge private information (which could be used to understand consumer behaviour by a keen marketer), they seek an audience, they are actors, they build their personal homepage, they market themselves (LinkedIn), they direct movies (YouTube), they become age experts (Blogs)... the list is endless. The tools they use to socialise are Facebook, Orkut, Twitter and scores of other networking sites. Social Media provide a base for businesses to pick up online conversations and turn them into leads.

What are Social Media?

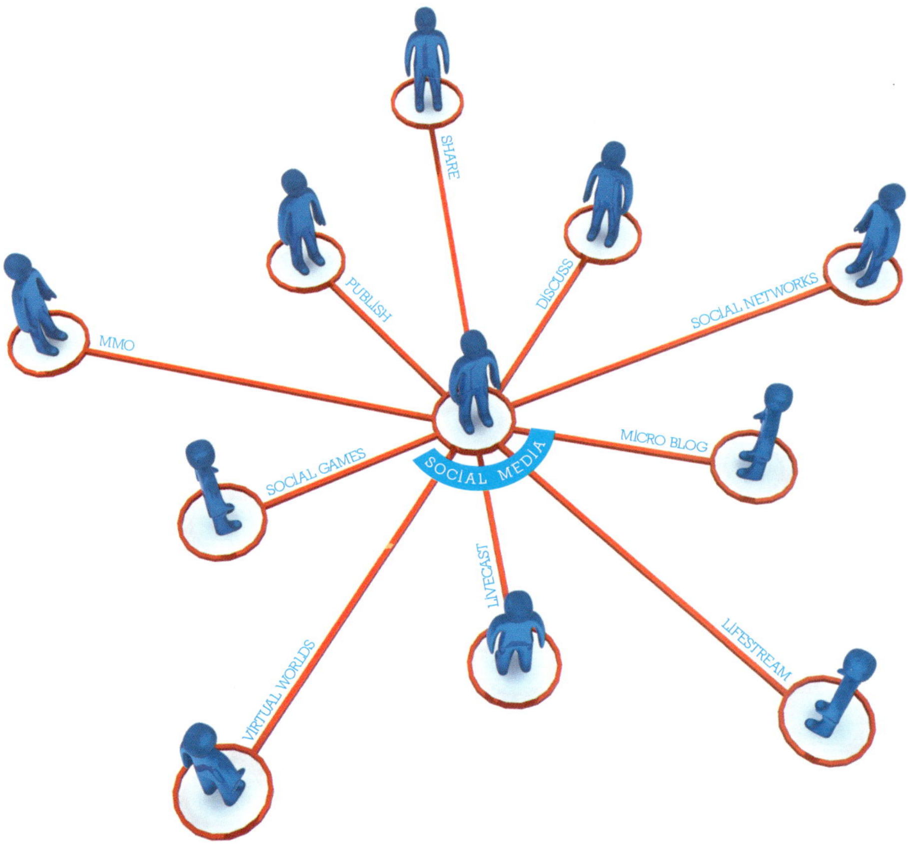

Social Media is a place to Socialize.

Social Media use web-based technology to quickly disseminate knowledge and information to a huge number of users. They allow creation and exchange of user-generated content. Facebook, Twitter, Hi5, Orkut and other social networking sites are collectively referred to as social media.

What is in it for brands?

For a brand, Social Media are all about online conversations. These conversations form a huge market place for brand engagement.

The stakeholders in these powerful conversations could be anybody - customers, employees, investors, critics, fans and competition.

Anyone who has Internet access and an opinion is a player in this marketplace.

These conversations are a market place where everything is discussed - customer queries, complaints and product reviews. Brand perceptions are altered, formed and re-established. These market places have become a place to advertise, a place to get into conversations, a place to defend brand reputation.

Some Benefits of Social Media

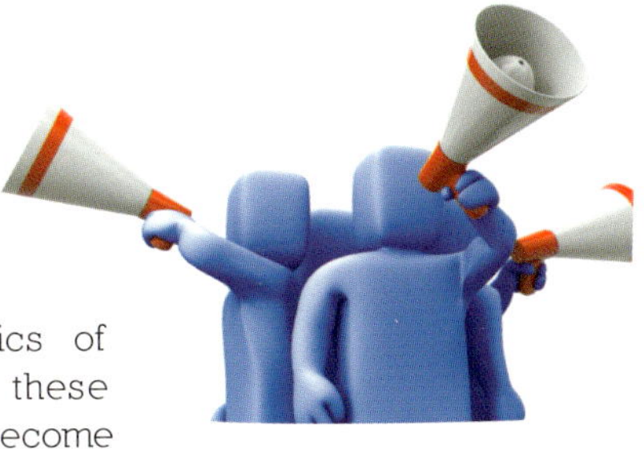

- Brand Reach & Awareness
- Consumer interaction through transactions, referrals
- Reputation Management

Due to the inherent characteristics of participation and openness of these conversations, Social Media have become immensely popular and they have evolved from small communities to becoming a market place for brands.

These communities, formed by like and unlike-minded people, have become a hotspot for discussion and the topics discussed are limitless. Most of the so-called expert content which was hitherto the privilege of trained professionals is being shared by a pool of freelancers gratis.

It's no wonder that the accuracy of Wikipedia is only marginally lower than Britannica Encyclopaedia.

Potential for brand reach through social networks in India

Social Networking:[Figures for India]

Social Network	Unique Users	Monthly Page Views
Orkut	16.8 million	1905 million
Facebook	14.6 million	1587 million
YouTube	14.5 million	500 million
LinkedIn	2.86 million	68.4 million
Flickr	1.70 million	10.1 million

Source: vizisense, Mar 2010

2 Debunking Social Media Myths

Myth 1

"If I am on Facebook, I have taken care of Social Media"

Facebook is a good start but it does not encompass Social Media in its entirety. One can say it is just the tip of the iceberg. There are many other tools of Social Media which allow us to collaborate, share and respond.

What are the basic forms of Social Media?

Social Networks

Social networks allow people to build personal web pages and then connect with friends to share content and communicate. E.g. Orkut, Facebook, MySpace, Hi5.

These social networks provide targeted advertising, and their huge user base makes them an ideal market place for various brands.

Facebook (400 million active users), Orkut (100 million active users). (source – www.vizisense.com)

The successful Barrack Obama election campaign employed various Social Media tools including Facebook to forge deep and meaningful conversations with people across states.

Most people use their social networks for information search as well. By socializing one can garner interesting facts in communities like Orkut. This makes social networks the most sought after media vehicle. Facebook has become an online yellow page directory.

Blogs

Blogs or web logs are online journals, where you write for a host of people eager to consume your information and experiences in the form of text, images and videos. These sites allow great room and great versatility.

How do I create an interesting and linkable blog?

- Personal brands, which can in turn add value and credibility to the corporate brand can be created through blogs.
- The blog should not be based on the company's achievements alone. The copy should be made personal, entertaining and give users a reason to return.
- The blog title and headlines should be catchy and creative.

Many bloggers have a huge fan following and are opinion leaders in their area of expertise. Apart from the immediate influencees (family, friends) bloggers have immense influence over potential buyers of products or services.

Wikis

Wikis allow one to not only post and access content but also revise and update content. Wikis add a new dimension to information-sharing by giving a new meaning to the term 'shared workspace'.

Wikipedia has become the first source of information for students and professionals alike. It is an easy and accessible resource for primary research. Companies like GE have an internal Wikipedia for their employees.

Content Communities

There are different community groups which share a specific kind of content. For example, Flickr is formed around sharing photographs and YouTube is a video sharing community.

Like social networks, one has to register, get a home page and make connections with friends. However, they are focused on sharing a particular type of content.

Microblogging

Social networking combined with bite-sized blogging, where small amounts of content ('updates') are distributed online and through the mobile phone network. Twitter is the clear leader in this field.

Podcasts

Podcasts are audio or video files that users can subscribe to. They are published on the Internet and it is the subscription feature that makes podcasts so powerful as a form of Social Media.

When a new podcast is posted to the web, all the subscribers' podcast services (such as iTunes) are automatically notified and hence get downloaded to their computer's hard drive. One can either listen to podcast on the computer system or download to an external MP3 drive such as an iPod.

Forums /Groups

Forums commonly exist around specific topics and interests, for example cars or music. Each discussion in a forum is known as a thread, and many different threads can be active simultaneously.

This makes forums good places to find and engage in a variety of detailed discussions. Forums can be places for lively, vociferous debate, for seeking advice on a subject, for sharing news, for flirting, or simply for whiling away time with idle chat.

The sites are moderated by an administrator, whose role it is to remove unsuitable posts or spam. A major difference between a forum and a blog is that a moderator won't be leading or guiding the discussion.

Blogs have a clear owner, whereas a forum's threads are started by its members.

A peep into popular social networks

Today consumers feel the need to be a part of a collective work that is directed towards common goals and they have an inherent tendency of seeking acknowledgement and appraisal. This need can be fulfilled by social media by engaging people in interesting activities online as they upload, find, share and participate.

Orkut

The inherent human need to make friends led to the popularity of this social network. In India it still takes courage to initiate a conversation with a stranger. Orkut solved this need and hence its use spread like wildfire.

Facebook

Contacts can be imported from Outlook, Windows Live contacts, or searched via a specific school, university or company. The site also recommends new connections based on one's own network and information.

- One's profile can contain a link to the company's website.
- One can post new material at least twice a week, and join and participate in groups, events; notes, photos and features can be used to keep the page current.
- A business page can be created in addition to the personal page by simply clicking on "Advertising" at the bottom of any Facebook page, then "Pages", and "Create a page."

LinkedIn

This is the site to reach a skilled audience, as it allows networking among professionals.

- The company recommends new contacts once one enters company information. One can also find connections by importing e-mail/address book connections.
- One's profile can contain a link to one's company's site.
- Other apps allow one to upload and share presentations, collect data for polls and more.

YouTube

Best for viral marketing based on innovative videos

- Videos created by one's company can be posted to an audience of millions.
- The website can be linked or embedded in one's site or blog. This directs viewers to one's company.

Flickr/ Picasa

Shares visual content in a way that engages viewers.

- Pictures and videos can be uploaded and shared.
- These can be organized and tagged, which makes them easier for others to find.
- One can join groups and create new contacts as one becomes more involved in the site.

Twitter

One of the most popular social networking sites is Twitter which allows one to use a completely different tool called microblogging. Through Twitter, one can reach the masses very easily and effectively. It has become a preferred advertising medium.

MySpace

Wove its magic by touching people through its music services offering. There are more than three million bands and musicians registered on MySpace, aiming to attract fans from among the 250 million members.

As the name suggests, social networks bring a large number of people from different nations, regions and professions under one umbrella. They create their profile page, connect with other people through inviting them or by accepting their requests and share content amongst all.

It is imperative to understand that today, Social Media have exponential potential. They are part of an ever-growing online network of people who discuss, comment, participate, share and create. A rough estimate can be made from the following table which suggests Social Media's popularity in terms of numbers that keep multiplying everyday.

Therefore, the faster you catch up with Social Media, the better you capture the live markets.

Myth 2

"Social Media are just a fad"

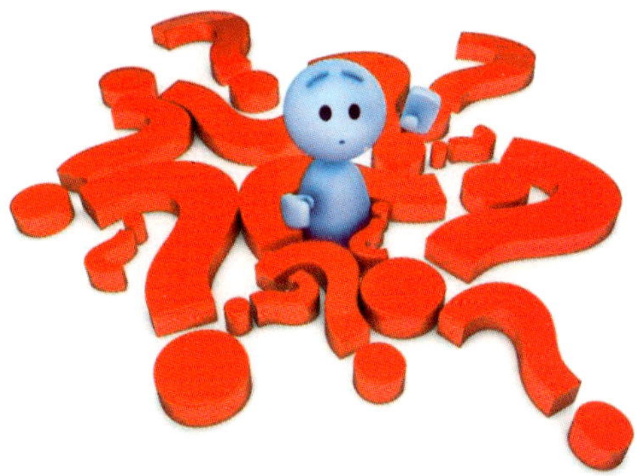

Why are social networks formed?

The networks are created to entertain and expand sharing and collaboration. The need to create networks arises out of human want to feel a part of something important and something bigger which is in fact, the essence of Social Media. Every individual has a desire to be a part of something important.

Also the fact that young people comprise a major chunk of social networks is evidence that social media is here to stay and their popularity is increasing day by day. According to a survey by Dentsu India that was conducted across 58 cities with 1734 respondents aged 25 years old or below, Internet usage dominates the second half of their day where it becomes their preferred medium of communication.

They are also most attentive while using the Internet. Social networking (34%), photo sharing (20%) and blogging (15%) are the most popular online activities of young people.

While on social networking sites 41% of Indian youth like uploading photos on their social networking profiles, 39% use it to communicate with friends and 8% install applications, implying that they like sharing content and communicating with friends.

Social Network	Focus	User Base
Facebook	General – connecting friends	400,000,000
Orkut	General. Owned by Google Inc. Popular in Brazil and decreasingly, in India	100,000,000
Twitter	General. Micro-blogging, RSS, updates	75,000,000
LinkedIn	Business and professional networking	53,000,000
Flickr	Photo sharing, commenting, photography related networking	32,000,000
LiveJournal	Blogging	17,564,977
Idiva	Fashion, Beauty, Relationship	340,000

What are the key factors driving Social Media?

Emotional need/desire to be heard

Now the playground and hangout den have come online. These days, very strong friendships are forged online. Social networking sites such as gurl.com have become online mentors providing relationship counselling and a place to connect with girls dealing with the same issues and concerns.

Need to create and make change

Social Media have also given rise to news sites solely created by citizens. Blogging has helped people to create a fan following; there is no need to advertise or promote oneself through conventional media. Facebook, Orkut and Blogger have empowered people to be the change.

Quest for Authenticity

People have become evolved consumers, and hence research everything about the product or service before making a final purchase.

Advertising in many cases does not have any effect on the consumer's decision-making process. People are more informed. Also Social Media have brought about a kind of openness and transparency, as barriers dissolve and anyone and everyone participates as a vigilant citizen journalist, a critic, an expert or an amateur photographer.

Social Media help in lead generation, brand awareness, increase in transaction numbers and increase one's reach. Which business doesn't want these goals to be achieved?

Pepsi, Coke, Nokia and many of the top brands have effectively used Social Media for achieving their business objectives.

Myth 3

"Social Media might work well for some industries but not for us"

Why should brands embrace Social Media in their marketing mix?

Limitations of Traditional Media

While mass media was successful in reaching any given target group in earlier times, today that's not the case. With the growth of mass media, consumers of today have too many choices and thus brands often fail to develop a deeper relationship with them. As Social Media evolve from the web 1.0 generation to web 2.0 generation, as emails make way for podcasts , web sites for RSS, shared workspaces for wikis, instant messaging for mash ups and enterprise directory for bookmarking we see a lot of innovation taking place in ways of collaboration and information sharing.

Social Media win trust of the consumers

These new media win the trust of consumers by connecting at a deeper level. One's peers become influencers for the brand. Therefore it is important to identify influential sites and the people who use these sites. The target audience can actually act as a brand ambassador if the brand can connect to them as individuals, to resonate with their needs and build their trust through transparency.

Connection between the new markets and companies

A method to connect people with markets outside the organization and within the organization is to hyper link. These networks create a more informed market place/consumer through the conversations being held. Most of the time, the information available in the market place is far more relevant than that available in the organization itself.

Competition

A close look at the most popular Social Media channels (Facebook, Orkut, Twitter, LinkedIn, Wiki, YouTube) will show a dedicated section for the biggest as well as the smallest brands on this new media. One cannot afford to have no presence on these channels if one's competitor is making waves with its products and services.

Online Brand Attack

Online channels have empowered people to have their say and share their opinions with an information-hungry world. Negative sentiment around a brand is a sure way to dilute the good work done earlier. The immediate effect of negative word-of-mouth on the Internet is the sliding stock price of the brand. By employing Reputation Management tools brands are better positioned to divert the danger or handle it in a much better way.

What could Social Media do for your brand?

- Learn what people are saying about you - Reputation Management.
- Create buzz for events and campaigns - Social Networks (Facebook, Twitter, Orkut).
- Identify and recruit influencers to spread your message - Partner with Social Media Specialists.
- Find new opportunities and customers - LinkedIn, Social Networks.
- Improve your search engine visibility - SEO (Search Engine Optimization), SEM (Search Engine Marketing), LPO (Landing Page Optimization).
- Gain competitive intelligence - Social Monitoring Tools
- Get your message out fast - Integrate your brand site with Social Media.

Why should your business be connected via Social Media?

Branding and Buzz Creation- Try and create a recognizable identity for your product or service, which is of high importance for a small-sized business. Get the word out about your products and services in a way that promotes online conversation.

Online Reputation Management- You are being talked about in various websites, forums and blogs. Each voice is important so keep a track of, analyze and respond to it. Try and fix if there is any wrong perception floating around.

Establish yourself as an expert- Use forums and message boards to answer questions professionally, honestly, and correctly, which will earn you respect as an expert in your niche. And then people online will look forward to your answers.

Word of mouth/word of mouse- Customers need to trust before purchasing - people trust their friends and loved ones more than anyone else. And since people share their opinions online, chances of someone buying your product or services become brighter when suggested by a trustworthy source. Build strategies through which people can talk positively about your product/services and spread the word.

Build relationships through personalization- Personalize your product or service offering: With innumerable choices in the hands of consumer, it has become imperative to add personal touch to your offering.

Your customers do play a vital role- Create situations where users get a chance to talk about your product/services. Let them like, dislike, suggest on any Social Media platform. This will also give you an idea of how you can modify or better your products and services.

Online Arbitration- One of the reasons some businesses are apprehensive about Social Media is because they're afraid of negative comments. But, if you take a close look, Social Media is just a way for you to realize how your products are perceived and take measures to establish a positive outlook for your brand. So, never ignore the communications of Social Media. Ignoring them will not contain the damage. But, when you reply, you are seen as a business owner who cares, who wants to make the customer happy, and that you're human.

What are the core offerings of Social Media for your brands?

How to benefit from the Social Media- integration and solutions

1. Create a website which has ample share options and where there is a platform for the users to comments and give feedback. A "share this" feature on your Home Page is an easy way out.

2. Keep your users updated with the latest developments in your company. Post links (press releases, articles or events) on the home page.

3. Make your presence felt in Twitter, YouTube and Flickr and reach a larger audience base.

4. Regularly post URLs via ping.fm on various social networking sites. Make your company an active participant online.

5. Making use of RSS feeds and updating your info is a great way to stay active.

Immediate Benefit: Whenever people initiate search (through various Social Media tools) your brand mention will pop up. Social Media companies design their website to generate more traffic by including hyperlinks, i.e links to and from Facebook,Twitter et al). By integrating the brand homepage and its content with Social Media tools, companies get wider reach amongst prospective consumers during various searches employed by users.

The best way to deal with a negative comment is to be open and put across your point of view. Today's consumers are far more informed.

Myth 4

"Deleting negative comments is the positive way"

Online Reputation Management

Online Reputation Management, or ORM, is the practice of consistent research and analysis of one's personal or professional, business or industry reputation as represented by the content across all types of online media.

Social Media is a common place for people to voice their opinions which are then read and spread by many others.

An organization can get to know all the positive and negative brand news and can act accordingly.

Sites to monitor online reputation:

- Google.com/alerts- Subscribe for this service via e-mail or RSS, and updates about you or your company can be sent directly to your inbox.
- Technorati.com- The largest blog search engine in the world. It can track any blog that links up to yours and send you RSS updates when someone is talking about your company.
- Backtype.com- If searching for your company amidst blog comments is your concern, this is the site for you.
- Search.twitter.com- Use this to search for any tweets related to your business.
- Trackur.com- It scours the Internet and provides extras (like charts and filters) that other sites don't.

If someone is talking badly about you or your company, instead of simply taking offence and dwelling on negative comments, address them and take the criticism for what it's worth: a chance to grow and learn.

Points of Action

A brand monitoring tool scours the entire web for mentions of your brands in various blogs and user communities. The brand buzz is then categorized as per your agreement with your Social Media partner. It could be as general as positive, negative and neutral sentiments or as specific as to which user is spreading negativities about your brand.

The important conversations are grouped under various heads as per the seriousness of the incidents so that you can take remedial action.

Brand monitoring is slowly picking up in Indian companies; many brands have a dedicated budget for this niche Social Media program.

Before deep diving in Social Media programs, it is best to deploy free Social Media tools to understand the overall sentiments about your brand.

Social Media tools to listen to conversations about your brand

Google Alerts

http://www.google.com/alerts

Google Alerts cover "News", "Web", "Blogs", "Groups" and "Video".

A Google alert lets you know if:

- News search - New articles make it into the top ten news results.
- Web search - New Web pages appear in the top twenty results.
- Blog search - New blog posts make it into the top ten results
- Groups search - New group posts make it into the top fifty results.
- New videos make it into the top ten results for your Google Video search.
- A sixth type of Google Alert, "Comprehensive", combines the results of the Google Alerts for "News", "Web" and "Blogs".

Setting up Google Alerts means you get updates automatically as they happen without having to run manual searches repeatedly yourself.

Google Trends

http://www.google.com/trends

Google Trends delivers charts that show how often a particular search term or terms are entered relative to the total search volume across regions of the world, and in various languages.

Popularity is broken down by region, city and language, and it's possible to refine the main graph by region and time period.

Google Blog Search

http://blogsearch.google.com

Use this tool to search amongst pools of blogs around the globe. Google Blog Search can be initiated simply by entering keywords and phrases in the search box, or honed with the advanced search facility available from the Google Blog Search homepage.

Technorati

http://www.technorati.com

The first blog search service, Technorati is still considered by many to be the best. It spiders and indexes over 112 million blogs, the results can be sorted by "authority" and "rank".

Delicious

http://del.icio.us

del.icio.us

Delicious is the first social bookmarking website and searching it gives you an idea of what people are bookmarking.

Other popular social bookmarking services include StumbleUpon, Magnolia.

Digg

http://www.digg.com

A social news service, Digg describes itself as follows: "Everything on Digg - from news, videos, images and podcasts-is submitted in our community. Once something is submitted, other people see it and Digg what they like best. If your submission is popular and receives enough Diggs, it is promoted to the front page for the millions of our visitors to see."

Other social news services include Reddit and Newsvine.

Classification of Listening tools

Brand Monitoring	Brand Mentions	Blog Buzz	Trends
Radian6	Google News Alerts	Google Blog Search	Google Trends
Trackur	Yahoo News	IceRocket	Google Insights for Search
Nielsen BuzzMetrics	How Sociable	BlogPulse	Trendrr
BrandsEye	Socialmention	Backtype	Serph

Number of page views, web traffic, sales conversions and number of downloads, and Social Media Campaign Service Level Agreements will make you believe otherwise.

Myth 5

"Measuring Social Media results is impossible"

10 Social Media tracking and analytics tools

No one can deny the fact that today Social Media are a great source of valuable marketing tools. But tracking Social Media could be relatively new for many people. Make sure that you keep a track of the scores in Social Media.

For example, a business would like to track what is being discussed about its brand across the web-are they creating a buzz or criticizing the product? So here, by tracking the most vital conversations about the business product/service, you have a better chance to identify the influential people in the niche, and get to figure out the best way to work on the flaws in the product/service plan.

Social Mention

If you ever wonder about tracking what people are saying about you all across the web, then Social Mention is the answer. It's a search and analysis platform that collects content from across the globe into one stream of information. Through this you can easily track comments about your company/products/services. More than 100 Social Media properties, including Twitter, Facebook, FriendFeed, Digg, YouTube, are tracked through this tool. Opt for Social Mention for point-in-time search and analysis, alerts, and API.

Bit.ly

This is a web tool that shrinks long URLs, and has statistical tools to track down the popularity of shortened links. Sometimes serious work could be fun and Bit.ly is a perfect example. Simply shorten long URLs and track the real time clicks easily.

SocialToo

SocialToo can help you be a social networking power user. It lets you keep your follower lists in sync across networks, and learn more about your relationships. Features include-creating surveys and sending them to multiple networks, tracking Social Media stats, auto follow, auto filtering and much more. You will also get daily e-mail on who is following you and who unfollows you on Twitter.

Twitteranalyzer

It is an interesting tool that helps to get all kinds of statistical charts about you and your friends' behaviour on Twitter. Some features of this tool are similar to Google Analytics. Some of its exciting features are - you can see how many followers are online presently, who retweets your messages, what people are writing about you, Twitter following stats, your Tweeting habits and many more.

Xinureturns

This is one of the best Social Media tracking tools to get a dashboard overview of your website on social networks and search engines. To get comprehensive info on Social Bookmarks, Technorati, Indexed Page, Google Pagerank, Ranking- all you have to do is to run this report.

Tweetstats

Tweetstats helps you analyze your tweets in various ways in the form of graphs. You will receive a graphic representation of your tweets/hour, tweets/month, tweet timeline and reply statistics. Now if you wish to have a graph of "Today's Top 10 Twitter Apps" and "Today Top @'ed Tweeps", you can do so easily. To run a check on which are the words that you use the most in your tweets, go to TrendCloud.

Twitalyzer

Twitalyzer is a free tool to evaluate the activity of any Twitter user and report on dozens of useful measures of success in Social Media. This is a very effective tool that gives a straight report on the behaviour of the user through his/her virtual influence and use of other tools. Links to URLs, the signal-to-noise ratio, clout, generosity and the tendency to share good info can be gauged easily.

BlogPulse

This is a very effective tool for "buzz tracking". Blog Pulse Trend Search allows you to create graphs that visually track "buzz" over time for certain key words, phrases or links and compare search terms/links in isolation, or use all three fields to compare search terms/links against others. You can use the Trend search to create your own graphs that plot "buzz" about specific search terms (issues, people, companies, brands, sports, etc.) in the blogosphere. You can also choose from three different time parameters- one month, two months or six months.

PostRank

Originally known as AideRSS it monitors and collects social engagement events correlated with online content in real-time across the web. It collects all the story-generated comments, bookmarks, tweets and various other forms of discussion from different Social Media platforms. Use PostRank facility to collect information and use it for a more targeted communication.

Broadtracker

Forums are exhaustive and sometimes you lose complete track of your presence on the threads. BoardTracker.com is the exact solution to clear such confusions. It's a forum search engine tool through which you can effectively track all the alerts, comments and other activities on the threads you are related to. You will never miss a point of discussion and you'll be able to streamline information right in front of you.

3 Executing Social Media Plans

Social Media implementation plan

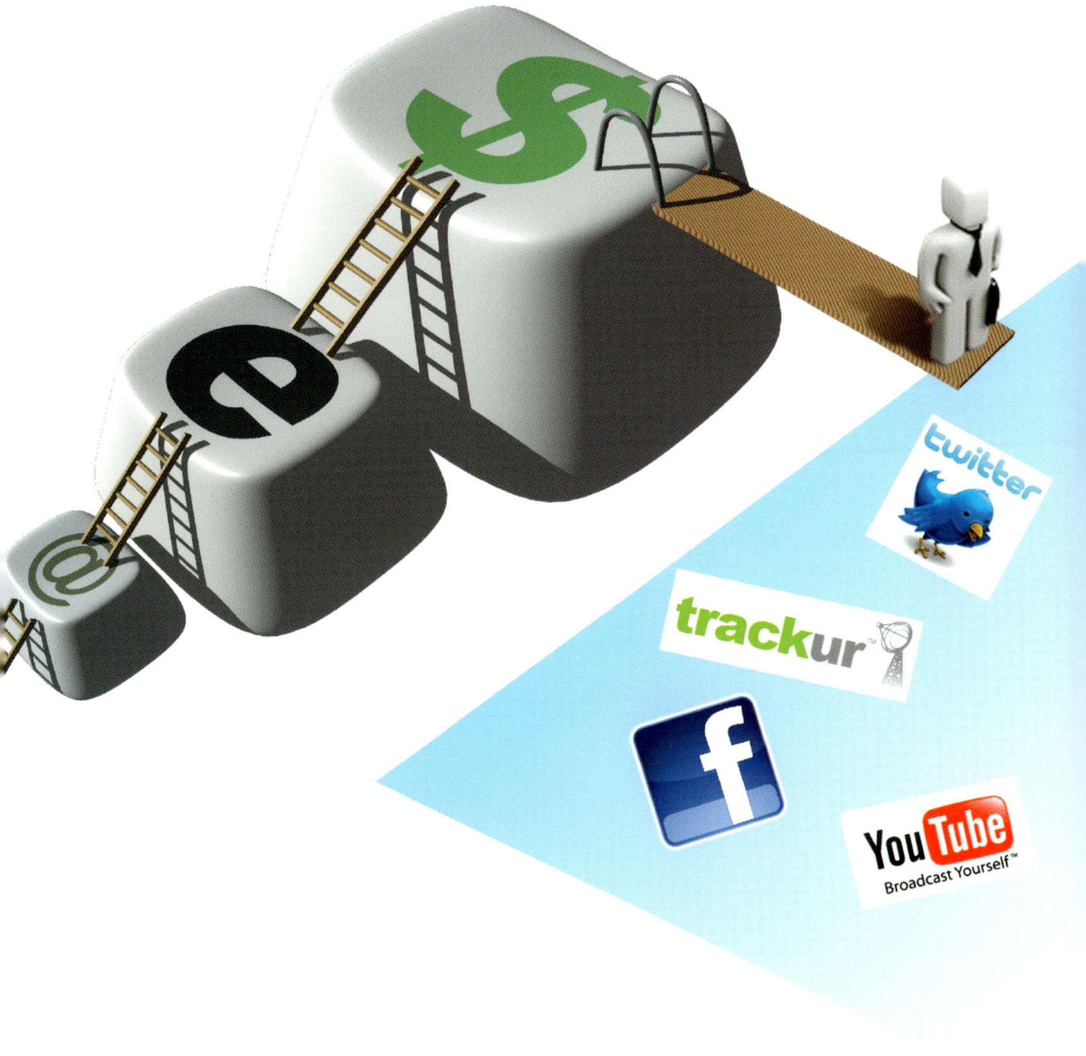

How do you implement Social Media programs?

Social Media Implementation is a 4-stage process.

1. The first step is to learn about the potential of various Social Media tools. Many of us use Social Media even without realizing it.

2. The second step is to identify business activities which need Social Media.

3. The third step is choosing and mapping various Social Media tools with the business activities with relevant content strategies.

4. And finally you need to measure Social Media Effectiveness through pre-defined measurement metrics.

Learn

- Social Media briefing workshop-Social Media orientation program for various business heads to learn the new media.

Identify

- Where are you stacked against your competition?
- What is your share of voice in the category?
- Identify business needs of various departments - Marketing ,Public Relations, Sales and so on.
- List the business concerns which you want Social Media to tackle.

Map

- Map business needs to various Social Media tools.
- Set goals and benchmarks for your Social Media program.
- Define Service Level Agreements with your Social Media Partner.

Measure

- Measure the number of lead generations, transactions, web traffic and increase in customers at regular intervals.
- Review the Social Media Program and update your Social Media Mix.

Making the best use of Social Media

After you've known all the methods and have established your profile in various websites, it's time to broadcast yourself in the best possible manner and reach out to a large audience.

Techniques to extract the maximum out of Social Media

Solo advertising isn't of much utility

Make sure that you are not the only one in a particular platform discussion about yourself. If there are a few more players from the same category then it becomes easier for users to read, compare and conclude. Therefore, post more articles from sources like Alltop (for industry-specific articles) and make people talk about it.

Use budURL

Apart from shortening your URL, this tool keeps a complete track of the visitors who are reading your content on various platforms. It will give you a fair idea of the total traffic and help you find out what is working and what is not.

Build relationships on each and every site

Posting information is not enough. In fact, it will do nothing for you or your brand. What you need to do is encourage users to involve themselves, participate and communicate further on the same lines. Talk to your users, go by their opinions when you think they make sense, collect feedback and then you'll come to know what effect the exercise has on your brand.

Blogs: get your posts out to a larger audience

Do not restrict your content and information to just a blog, But try and reach out to a larger audience base. You can do this effectively through ping.fm and also track your numbers via budURL.

Other option: pingvine.com enables your blog's RSS feed to automatically update ping.fm (thus, less work for you). One problem you may face while integrating the entire set up is that you will not be able to use budURL in tandem with this site; therefore tracking the number of visitors won't be possible.

Measuring the Immeasurable

One of the most challenging tasks for a Social Media strategist is convincing businesses on their return on investment from Social Media programs.

Most of the activities of Social Media have non-financial impact such as:

- Website Visitors
- Impressions
- Customer complaints
- Positive press
- Retweets
- YouTube views
- Positive WOM
- Facebook friends
- Social Mention
- Blog comments
- Visitors to brick and mortar stores
- Delivered e-mails

It is necessary to plug these activities into business benefits such as Return on Investment by charting baseline metrics before the launch of a Social Media program.
The frequency, reach and yield will showcase the return on investment (Increased sales, transactions, enquiry, lead generations etc).

This exercise will also provide concrete proof that the concept is working.

Request for Proposal

How do you measure influence?

General trends to measure influence are some of the parameters we use to determine which bloggers and networkers to focus on.

- Traffic - Unique visitors, page views, RSS subscribers.
- Inbound Links - Primarily contextual links from well-ranked sites and blogs.
- Reader Engagement - Time spent on site, comments.
- Recommendations - Re-tweets, bookmarking, tagging and sharing of content.
- Connections - Number of followers/mutual connections across multiple social sites.
- Track Record - Age of domain, number of blog posts, length of engagement.
- Traffic Referred to your site or blog - Analytics tell which referring sites send the most traffic.
- Conversion rate of those visitors - Gives the rate of conversion for each referring site.

Social Media Request for Proposal

This is how information is exchanged between Client and Social Media Partner.

Client information

- Organization's background
  1. Company History
  2. Brand Vision
  3. Products & Services
  4. Markets Served
- What are your immediate and future business objectives?
- What are your key performance indicators?
- What are your key concern areas?
- What are your expectations from Social Media?
- Project Brief of Social Media
- Project Schedule and General Guidelines
- Service Level Agreements
- Measurement Metrics

A checklist for Social Media specialist's credentials

- Ownership structure
- Proprietary tools
- Years of experience
- Number of employees
- Single point of contact
- Campaigns executed
- Vendors employed
- Primary Social Media communication tools

What should you ask a Social Media Specialist prior to initiating a partnership?

1. What is your Social Media strategy?
2. Deliverables of the campaign - Service level agreement
3. What is your approach to Social Media Risk Management?
4. How do you incorporate existing applications, websites, microsite and newsletter programs into your overall Social Media strategy?
5. How do you ensure compliance with client legal requirements?
6. Please describe your approach to integrating across client marketing, customer service and corporate communications departments.
7. How do you integrate Social Media with Traditional Media?

Brand Reputation /Social Media monitoring process

1. What is your brand/reputation monitoring process (i.e. proprietary tools used, methodology, etc)?
2. What is your opinion on automated sentiment analysis?
3. How long (on an average) between a potential issue being posted online and being flagged to the client?
4. What volume of mentions has your organization handled in the past (e.g. 2,500 mentions per week)?
5. What is your quality assurance process to ensure that the large volumes of data gathered in the monitoring process are handled efficiently and representative of the overall online conversation?
6. What services do you provide in support of online crisis management?
7. Please provide a case study detailing your work for the purposes of managing reputation or online crisis management, including outcomes and lessons learned.

Metrics And Measurement

1. What methodology did you use for measuring the success of your Social Media Programs for clients? Kindly provide specific examples based on past work.

2. Have you developed any proprietary metrics and how have you applied these for clients?

3. How have you defined R.O.I. from a Social Media perspective in the past?

4. What will be your approach to server analytics and community analytics for program measurement?

5. Do you have the capability to measure cost per lead or cost per acquisition? Please provide an example of a project on which you have done so.

6. What platforms are you unable to measure accurately, or able to provide only limited measurements from?

7. Kindly provide a sample of a measurement document or final report (specifics should be removed).

Education

1. Do you offer Social Media Training Services for clients?
2. What format does your training take (i.e. workshops, presentations, walkthroughs, webinars/online learning)?
3. How do you measure progress and evaluate training effectiveness?
4. Kindly provide testimonials or feedback from training participants.

Call to action

- Learn Social Media-Social Media is not an option.
- Identify your brand's Key Performance indicators and pain points.
- Map your business requirements with Social Media programs.
- Measure your Return on Engagement.

How can corporate functions be married to Social Media tools?

Social Media tools empower all the stakeholders of the companies to benefit from one another. Various corporate functions could integrate most of the activities within the Social Media programs.

Corporate Function	Objective	Goals	Social Media Activities
Research	Listening	Customer knowledge, Competitive insights, Cost savings over focus group	Monitoring reports, Private communities, Digital vision development
Marketing	Engagement	Awareness and buzz, Time spent, Change brand perceptions, Purchase intent	Blog, Video blogs, Social network, Viral videos, Contests
Sales	Energizing	Community membership, Recommendations, Sales inquiries/ ideas	Brand communities, Influence outreach, Widgets
Customer Service	Support	Questions answered, Customer satisfaction, Avoided support calls	User communities, Wikis, Support forums, Loyalty programs, Observe reports
Product Development	Embracing	Product ideas generated, Speed of development	User communities, Suggestion boxes, Observe reports

Building a company with Social Media

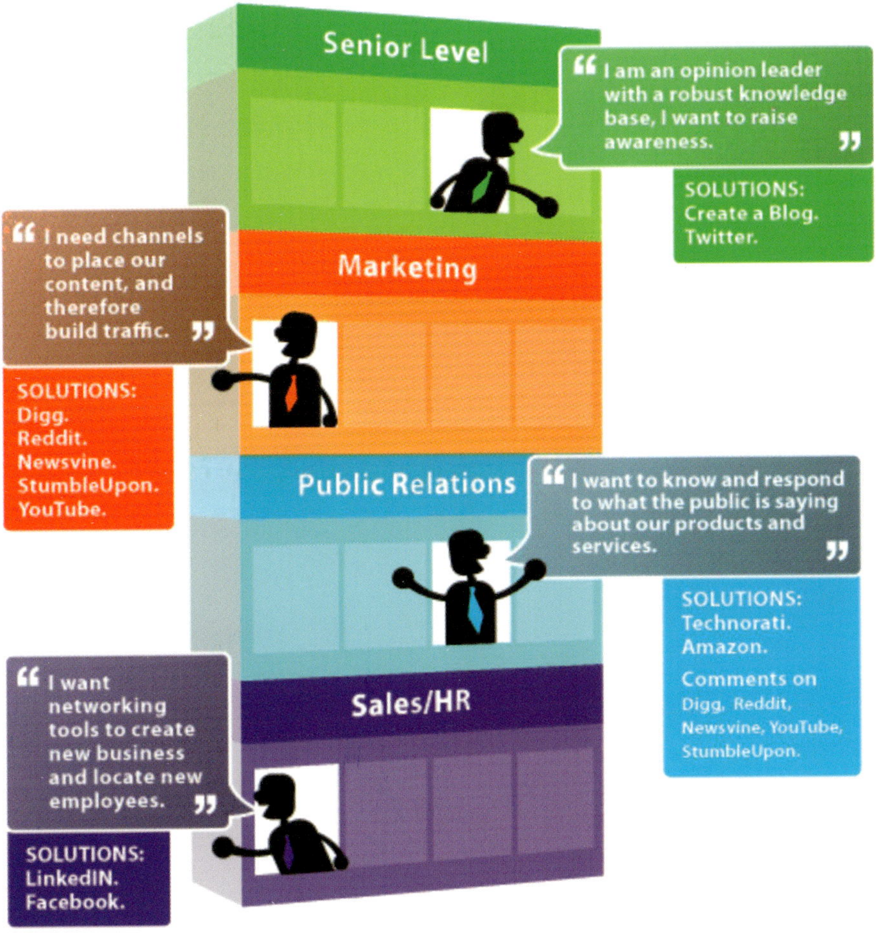

In a nutshell

- Social Media are a new initiative for reaching your customer at a phenomenally low cost.
- Social Media enable a customer to be a marketer for your brand.
- Social Media are measurable and provide targeted advertisement to your consumer.
- Social Media allow you to listen to what is being said about your brand, manage your brand through online reputation management and track and measure certain aspects of your brand.
- Tracking what is being said about you and your peers, Reputation management are some functions of social media that companies cannot afford to ignore.
- Social Media are a very crucial extension of business as they allow sharing of knowledge and insights, development of integrated business processes, and enable distributed business teams to work together closely to complete predefined tasks.

What we cannot forget

- As Social Media are real time, the content should be up-to-date and interesting.
- Social Media are meant to engage and interact with the Internet users and at no point of time should companies try and control their behaviour.
- Social Media should also be expandable to converge with other media so that it keeps in step with advances in technology.

4 Market Examples

Reputation Monitoring case study

Brand: XYZ

Activity: To monitor the sentiments surrounding XYZ products.

Dentsu Digital's offering:

- Monitored the conversations across the entire online media.
- Sorted out the most active incidents on various platforms.
- Installed and implemented web analytics.
- Evolved strategy for spreading positive word of mouth and remedial actions as per severity of incidents.
- Partnered with Social Media Influencer to increase brand sentiments.
- Built strategies to monitor and track negative influencer.

*XYZ- The name of ORM client is never revealed by an agency.

User generated Content Platform Creation

Brand: Aircel

Social Media Campaign: A dedicated website for people to come online and share their feelings for lonely senior citizens apart from donating old mobile phones.

Brand site: www.aircelsilence.com

VIEW COMMENTS

I 1 I 2 I 3 I 4 I 5 I 6 I 7 I
>>

"Who says the world only belongs to the youth? It is our parents and grandparents who have built it up for us. Let us respect and care for them"

-a mehta
2009-12-29 I 23:24:04

"We should keep old citizens safe and secure. They deserve all our love"

-sudeep
2009-12-29 I 23:19:49

"Yes... it's true "silence is not always golden". So be honest, good, humble & sincere towards all especially our old age citizens' because one day you all will reach same stage. So, be good & do good."

-Vikaram Brahma
2009-12-29 I 22:17:17

"A touching communication. Little things that we ignore can mean so much joy and happiness. Lets do our bit!"

-shitesh
2009-12-29 I 06:48:10

HelpAge India Fighting isolation, poverty, neglect

AIRCEL

Empowering traditional with digital media

Social Media Tools employed: Facebook, Blog, YouTube

- **Campaign**: Aircel's Save Our Tiger Initiative.
- **Campaign elements**: TVC, Print, Outdoor, Radio & Social Media.
- **Client**: Aircel.

Objective: To create a single platform where people can converge to pledge their support, a website www.saveourtigers.com was created. Social networking site Facebook and Twitter were used to provide a platform for all Indians who cared for this cause.

Consumer support for the cause: More than 2,16,000 users and counting.

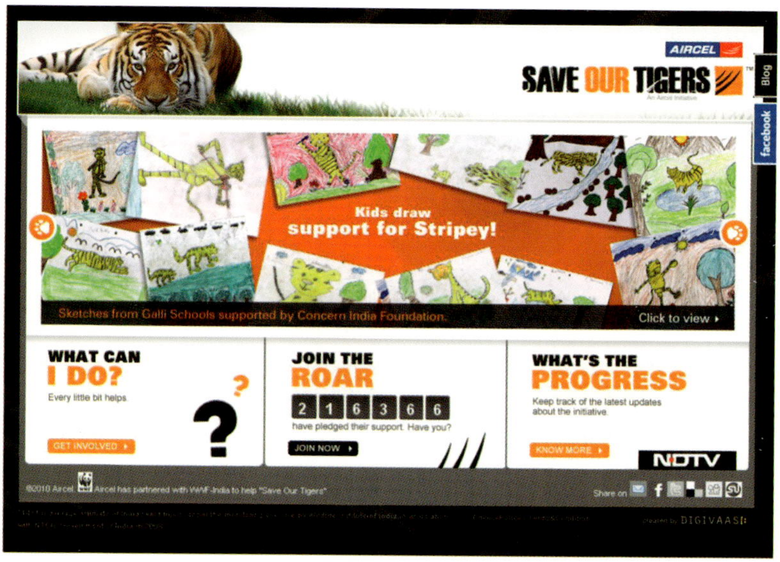

Dentsu Digital Social Media Products

Indian Fantasy League

www.indianfantasyleague.com/

The Concept

Indianfantasyleague.com gives you a unique opportunity to become team owners by selecting your dream team in cricket, football, tennis and golf. Register for free and start winning exciting prizes.

Inception Story: Launched the league in April '08 along with domestic Twenty20 cricket, initially it was focused on cricket. However, in due course it has started offering fantasy gaming options for Lawn Tennis, Football et al.

Apart from sports, IFL tied up with ET for offering stock fantasy game. Among other game offerings were a game for Olympics, general elections 2009.

With mobile phones becoming an identity for an individual, it was natural for IFL to provide mobile enabled fantasy gaming for consumers from February 2010.

What has it achieved?

- Within a month of launch, topped 1 million users, today over 3 million users.
- During IPL, 238,000 active playing teams.
- Today, over 500,000 team registrations.
- During IPL 08 hits from over 1800 Indian cities and towns.
- Today, hits from 2336 cities / Towns.
- Currently attracting users from 139 countries worldwide.
- Average time spent on the site at ~ 12 minutes per day which is double that of time spent on any other gaming site or social networking site.
- Today touching 40 million page views.

Garden of Love

www.gardenoflove.in

Title Sponsor: Aircel

The Concept

Romance moved to the mobile perhaps a decade ago when both boy and girl had this 24/7 device by their side. Now you could kiss and make up or just whisper a sweet nothing anytime of the day or night.

However, Valentine's Day which made a big India entry perhaps 15-20 years ago, has remained in the Archie's store mould ever since. SMS has made some inroads, but the medium lacks emotion, passion and most importantly any feeling of romance.

Garden of Love (GOL) is all that Valentines need. It has shape and form. It is easy to interact with, create, share, nurture and grow. It is an open demonstration of love when you want it loud and visible; it is protected and private when you want it so.

It is about flowers, it is about beauty; it is about loving and sharing.

The beauty of GOL is that it does not begin and end with Valentine's Day. A birthday, an anniversary, a simple "missing you", a promotion, a celebration, Mother's Day, Father's Day, everyone of them is an occasion to plant a flower and share your happiness with friends and family.

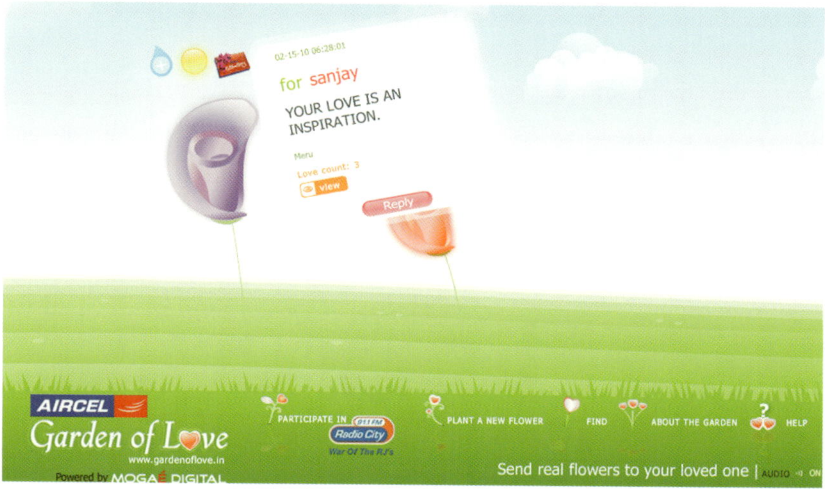

Cadbury's Social Media innovation in GOL

Cadbury used Social Media product Garden of Love to connect with its consumers in a very engaging way.

In GOL when one creates a flower for a friend, he has 3 options to keep the flower alive and dancing .

1. Water it - The water count shows along side the flower, indicating one's own looking after of the plant and also one's popularity amongst friends, who can also water the flower.

2. Give it sunlight.

3.Give it nourishment.

Cadbury's replaced the nourishment option with their brand initiative. The icon was replaced with their chocolate image. This was a brand-immersive move. User & friends could click on the Cadbury's pack and leave it as a sign of goodwill and friendship alongside the flower.

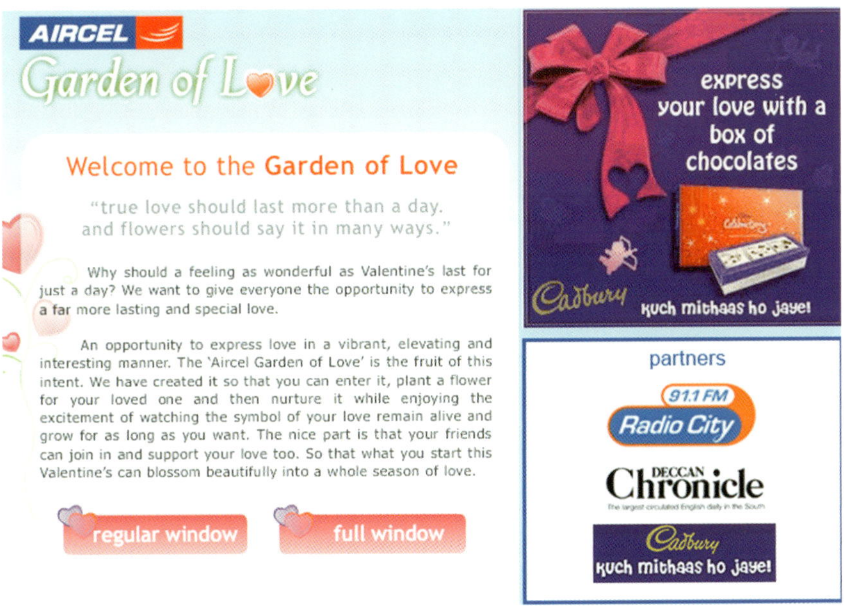

Examples from developed markets

Coca-Cola

Coca-Cola has used several ways such as blogging, sharing photos/videos, tweets, Social Media apps to promote their brands and achieved huge success.

Carol Kruse, Coca-Cola's Vice President of Global Interactive Marketing

I think before you have ROI you have to really understand how Social Media is driving your business. If you're a traditional sales funnel type of company and if you're selling something online, you could say, "I know how many sales I got out of that Social Media app." We are not a funnel company, but we still need to measure the value of what we do. I can't measure it in actual incremental sales because I'm not selling something online. It's much safer to say we are focusing on measuring the business value of different types of digital marketing.

In that context, we are asking whether it's driving brand health or brand love. Is it driving purchase intent? In some cases, like search and online advertising, we have been able to measure ROI driving true incremental volumes and true increases in sales. It's the same thing from a loyalty and CRM standpoint. We have a lot of online promotions and online loyalty programs like My Coke Rewards, and we've certainly measured the amount of true incremental volume those type of programs drive.

X-Men

Before the release of the movie X-Men-3, "Last Stand", the producers used a social networking site to promote it. All the users who added the X-Men profile as a peer received certain exclusive benefits. As a result of this media plan, almost 3 million members of the myspace.com community added X-Men as peer in just 1 month. The movie got a huge opening and it became the fourth-biggest movie in box office history.

Dell

Dell is usually known for the cost-effective methods that it uses and so it jumped into Social Media to reach people. Dell reported that offers on its Dell Outlet Twitter account have resulted in bookings worth over $3 million in revenue. This was attributable to its Twitter posts. It might sound like a small percentage for a company that books $16bn in revenue annually-but a nice number however, especially in a dreary economy.

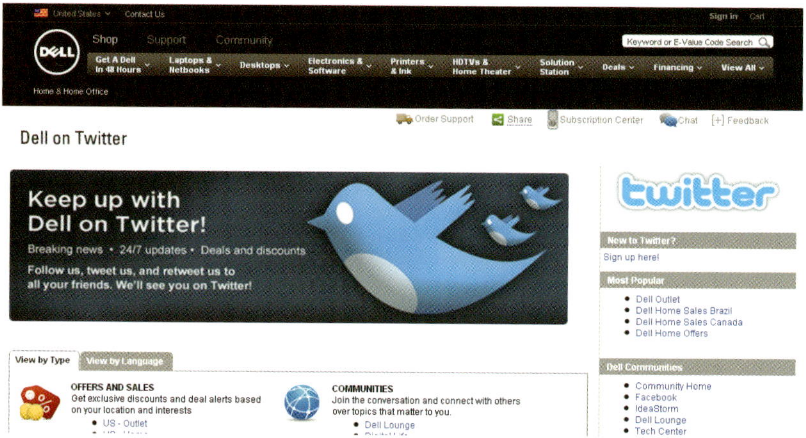

SAP

This third largest software company in the world faced a challenge in the year 2002. It wanted to become a platform company using NetWeaver. The company had to open its platform and allow the other developers to use the platform in order to solve their business problems. The company had to interact with several developers across the globe. With the use of innumerable Social Media tools the task became so much easier to execute. As a result of which, the company gained global collaboration and adoption of new SAP products increased.

HP

HP Social Media case study is another good example. HP Social Media managers engaged experts who work daily with customers to develop relevant marketing content grounded in true client need and real-life business issues. By combining podcasting with blogging and traditional tech-media syndication, HP now validates its messaging via an extensive buyer audience review process that yields vetted, relevant content that HP marketing can deploy in its ongoing sales and marketing efforts.

invent

Uniqlo's Uniqlock case study

Uniqlo

Uniqlo is a Japanese leading casual wear designer, manufacturer and retailer. The company also operates in China, South Korea, the UK, France, USA, and Singapore. As a part of its global campaign to express its fashionability, Uniqlo established the promotional website, "Uniqlock,".

Uniqlock

Uniqlock website was launched on 2007 by Uniqlo for its polo shirts later upgraded to cashmere sweaters in 2008. The website displays videos with Japanese girls dancing and a real-time digital clock. The website features a downloadable blog part, video sharing websites and cyber buzz. The campaign was followed by many other promotions like "Uniqlo Jump", "Uniqlo Today", "World Uniqlock" and "Uniqlo Grid".

Results

- Total views over 68 million times in 209 nations.
- Blogpart was installed over 27,000 times in 76 nations.
- Screensaver was downloaded over 175,000 times.
- Uniqlock campaign received the Grand Prix in the One Show and at the Clio Awards, in 2008.
- Sales through the brand's online store increased by 19% annually.

Innovative use of Four Square

- Foursquare is a location-based mobile social network based on a nightlife game where users get points for everything one does on the service like being the first to visit a new place, going out every night of the week etc.

- Foursquare provides a base platform centered on finding one's friends, sharing one's location via GPS and instant messaging.

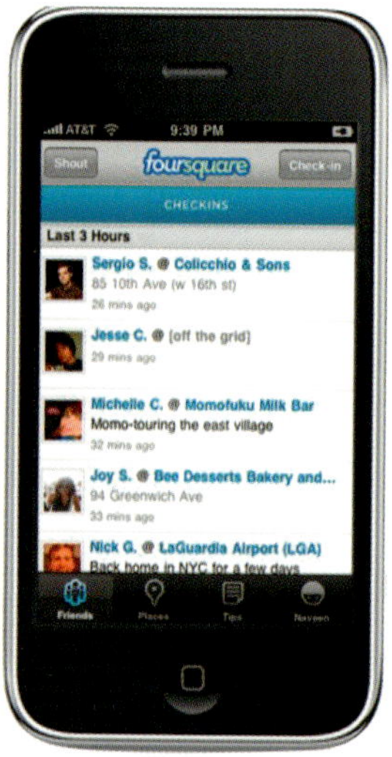

- It hinges on the popularity of video games - By creating a mobile social network bolstered by GPS into a fun challenge reinforced by incentives like a video game.

- In the app, one can update his location, send shouts to friends, track one's achievements and keep a to-do list that is shared with friends. One can also add additional information about favourite food or beer and favourite hangouts.

- Foursquare draws from a list of known restaurants, bars, and nightclubs and also integrates reviews from Yelp and Google Maps.

- Depending on points in the leader board, one can receive badges for special achievements. like being the 'mayor' of a certain place

PepsiCo Integration

- PepsiCo by integrating loyalty program with LBS gets live notifications, when its customers are close to targeted outlets and can present offers to them.

- PepsiCo is also introducing a LBS application called "Pepsi Loot".

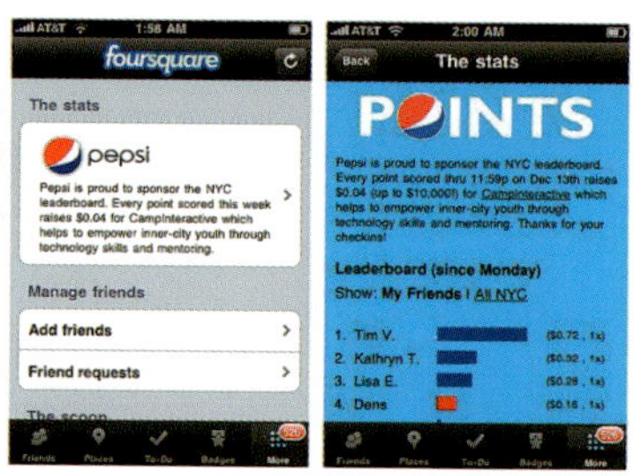

Social Media for social cause

Blog for the victims of the Chinese Earthquake

Forrester analyst Jeremiah Owyang has been using his blog to bring attention to the situation in China after the devastating earthquake which may have claimed over 50,000 lives. Jeremiah used his blog as a platform to inspire people to donate money to the Red Cross.

Social Media in Disasters

When disaster strikes, communication is often interrupted. In order to get assistance and aid into a disaster area in a safe and timely manner, an open line of communication is critical in a crisis.

But as other disasters and world events occur, technology and Social Media are being utilized more frequently in the relief effort. Friends and loved ones of victims frantically searching for information are now using wireless technology and social networking like Twitter, Facebook, Skype, Flickr and YouTube for information and assistance.

Text HAITI to 90999

This mobile fund-raising initiative, supported by the United States State Department, the joint effort between the American Red Cross, Mobile Accord and the mGive Foundation had raised more than $30 million.

Social Networks in Japan

MIXI

Mixi, launched in 2004, is the biggest social network in Japan. Mixi reports more traffic than Amazon Japan. The name supposedly refers to the fact that "I can mix" with other users.

Mixi's site design and navigation are extremely intuitive. One's homepage displays a selection of one's friends, a list of their latest blog posts and photos and the latest news from one's communities.

Mixi's profile pages are attractive , loads quickly and the site doesn't break. It's also interesting to note that the profile pictures on Mixi are rarely of the page owner: movie stars, cartoon characters, pets and brand logos seem to dominate.

GREE

GREE allows online users to share information, games and to look after online virtual pets.The word GREE comes from the phrase "Six degrees of separation". Their web based site includes a profile page, diary log, photo album, reviews, community section and mail. The service has been running since 2004.

The web based service looks fairly plain, but the banner for their mobile phone based site looks a lot more interesting.

Mobage town

Mobage-town is mobile Social network based on virtual world and gaming platform. Subscribers can exchange messages, chat in communities, share music, read pocket novels, and blog, among other things. The site's "killer feature", however, is the vast selection of free games that makes most users register in the first place.

Each of the 11 million Mobage-town members is represented by an avatar "living" in a virtual room. Both the characters and rooms can be pimped out with new clothes and wallpaper, for example. In order to do that, users must acquire "Moba Gold", a virtual currency from Mobage-town that generated great revenues.

Social Media Glossary

Blog

A blog is an online journal that's updated on a regular basis with entries that appear in reverse chronological order. Blogs can be about any subject. They typically contain comments by other readers, links to other sites and permalinks.

Cloud computing

Cloud computing (also called "the cloud") refers to the growing phenomenon of users who can access their data from anywhere rather than being tied to a particular machine.

Crowd sourcing

Crowd sourcing refers to harnessing the skills and enthusiasm of those outside an organization who are prepared to volunteer their time contributing content or skills and solving problems.

Digital inclusion

Digital inclusion, or e-inclusion, is an effort to help people who are not online gain access with affordable hardware, software, tech support/information and broadband Internet service, so they can begin to use this technology to improve their lives.

Digital story

A digital story is a short personal nonfiction narrative that is composed on a computer, often for publishing online or publishing to a DVD. They are told from the narrator's point of view and the subject is generally about something the maker experienced personally. Digital Stories typically range from two to minutes in length (though there are no strict rules) and can include music, art, photos, voiceover and video clips. They are also typically created by one person with little technical training, rather than by a team of professionals.

Feed

A Web feed or RSS feed is a format that provides users with frequently updated content. Content distributors syndicate a Web feed, enabling users to subscribe to a site's latest content. By using a news reader to subscribe to a feed, you can read the latest posts or watch the newest videos on your computer or portable device on your own schedule.

Flash mob

A flash mob is a group of individuals who gather and disperse with little notice for a specific purpose through text messages, Social Media or viral e-mails. It's now generally considered a somewhat dated term (already!).

GPS

GPS is shorthand for Global Positioning System, a global navigation satellite system. GPS-enabled devices - most commonly mobile handhelds or a car's navigation system - enable precise pinpointing of the location of people, buildings and objects.

Hosting

A blog, video or podcast needs a hosting service before it can appear online. Companies sometimes host their blogs on their own servers, but a better choice for video or audio is to use a host such as YouTube, Viddler or Magnify.net for video and a host such as Libsyn for podcasts.

Internet newsroom

An Internet newsroom also called Internet pressroom or online media center is an area of a corporate website that communicates corporate messages and makes content available to the news media and the public. Rather than just feature little-read press releases, a true Internet newsroom incorporates features such as videos, podcasts, high-resolution image galleries, surveys, forums, blogs and other online marketing communications materials.

Mashup

Mashups (or mash-ups) have several meanings. A music mashup is a combination of two or more songs, generally the vocals of one song overlaid on top of the melody of another. A video mashup is the result of combining two or more pieces of video, such as news footage with original commentary. A Web mashup results when a programmer overlays information from a database or another source on top of an existing website, such as homes for sale taken from Craigslist plotted on a Google Map.

Metadata

Metadata refers to information-including titles, descriptions, tags and captions-that describes a media item such as a video, photo or blog post. Some kinds of metadata-for example, camera settings such as exposure, aperture, focal length and ISO speed - can be captured automatically from the device without needing a human to enter the data.

Microblogging

Microblogging is the act of broadcasting short messages to other subscribers of a Web service. On Twitter, entries are limited to 140 characters, and applications like Plurk and Jaiku take a similar approach with sharing bite-size media.

Moblog

A moblog is a blog published directly to the Web from a phone or other mobile device. Mobloggers may update their sites more frequently than other bloggers because they don't need to be at their computers to post.

Open source

In its strict sense, open source refers to a software code that is free to build upon. But open source has taken on a broader meaning - such as open source journalism and open source politics - to refer to the practice of collaboration and free sharing of media and information to advance the public good. Well-known open-source projects include the Linux operating system, the Apache Web server and the Firefox browser.

RSS

RSS (Really Simple Syndication) - sometimes called web feeds - is a Web standard for the delivery of content - blog entries, news stories, headlines, images, video - enabling readers to stay current with favourite publications or producers without having to browse from site to site. All blogs, podcasts and videoblogs contain an RSS feed, which lets users subscribe to content automatically and read or listen to the material on a computer or a portable device.

Screencast

A screencast is a video that captures what takes place on a computer screen, usually accompanied by audio narration. A screencast is often created to explain how a website or piece of software works, but it can be any piece of explanatory video that strings together images or visual elements.

Search engine marketing

Search engine marketing (SEM) is a series of online tactics that, when combined with SEO, helps to attract customers, generate brand awareness and build trust. SEM (sometimes called search marketing) seeks to increase websites' visibility chiefly through the purchase of pay-per-click ads and paid inclusion.

Search engine optimization

Search engine optimization (SEO) is the process of arranging your website to give it the best chance of appearing near the top of search engine rankings. As an Internet marketing strategy, SEO considers how search engines work and what people search for. Optimizing a website primarily involves editing its content, identifying high-traffic keywords and improving the site's layout and design.

Smart phone

A smart phone (or "smartphone") is a handheld device capable of advanced tasks beyond those of a standard mobile phone. Capabilities might include email, chat, taking photos or video or hundreds of other tasks.

Social bookmarking

Social bookmarking is a method by which users locate, store, organize, share and manage bookmarks of Web pages without being tied to a particular machine. Users store lists of personally interesting Internet resources and usually make these lists publicly accessible. Delicious is the best-known social bookmark site.

Social capital

Social capital is a concept used in business, nonprofits and other arenas that refers to the goodwill and positive reputation that flows to a person through his or her relationships with others in social networks.

Social Media optimization

Social Media Optimization (SMO) is a set of practices for generating publicity through Social Media, online communities and social networks. The focus is on driving traffic from sources other than search engines, though improved search ranking is also a benefit of successful SMO.

Streaming media

Unlike downloadable podcasts or video, streaming media refers to a video or audio that can be watched or listened to online but not stored permanently. Streamed audio is often called Webcasting. Traditional media companies like to stream their programs so that they can't be distributed freely onto file-sharing networks.

Tags

Tags are keywords added to a blog post, photo or video to help users find related topics or media, either through browsing on the site or as a term to make your entry more relevant to search engines.

Tweet

A post on Twitter, a real-time social messaging system. While all agree on usage of tweet as a noun, people disagree on whether you "tweet" or "twitter" as a verb. RT stands for retweet: Users add RT in a tweet if they are reposting something from another person's tweet.

UGC

UGC stands for user-generated content, an industry term that refers to all forms of user-created materials such as blog posts, reviews, podcasts, videos, comments and more.

Web analytics

Web analytics is the measurement, collection, analysis and reporting of Internet data for the purpose of understanding who your visitors are and optimizing your website.

Web conferencing

Web conferencing is used to conduct live meetings or presentations over the Internet. In a web conference, each participant sits at his or her own computer and is connected to other participants via the Internet. This can be either a downloaded application on each of the attendees' computers or a web-based application where the attendees will simply enter a URL (website address) to enter the conference.

Webcasting

Webcasting refers to the ability to use the Web to deliver live or delayed versions of audio or video broadcasts. The chief distinctions between webcasting and traditional radio broadcasting include the following: Listeners can tune into webcasts from anywhere in the world, whereas radio broadcasting is generally local; webcasts may be "interactive" (for example, users may rewind the show) whereas radio broadcasting generally is not; listeners may receive textual or visual data (artist and song titles, ads, album artwork, etc.) during a webcast.

Webinar

Short for Web-based seminar, a webinar is a presentation, lecture, workshop or seminar that is transmitted over the Web. In general, participants register in advance and access the presentation in real time over the Internet and listen to the presenter either through computer speakers or a telephone connection. Webinars are generally one-way and can involve chat or polls. There are a large number of companies that offer webinar services.

Widget

A widget, sometimes called a gadget, badge or applet, is a small block of content, typically displayed in a small box, with a specific purpose, such as providing weather forecasts or news, that is constantly updating itself (typically via RSS). Widgets make it easy to add dynamic content to your site or blog.

Wiki

A wiki is a collaborative website that can be directly edited by anyone with access to it. Small teams often find that they can accomplish a task more easily by creating a collaborative online workspace using wiki software such as pbworks, Socialtext or mediawiki.

Wikipedia

Wikipedia is a Web-based, multi-language, free-content encyclopedia written collaboratively by volunteers. Sponsored by the non-profit Wikimedia Foundation, it has editions in about 200 different languages.

Word-of-mouth marketing

Word-of-mouth marketing, sometimes called grassroots marketing or conversational marketing, is an umbrella term for dozens of techniques that can be used to engage and energize customers. By building relationships with influencers through WOM, marketers can get people to become so enthusiastic about a cause, product or service that they drive sales through conversations.

Conclusion

Social Media provide marketers with a new platform to reach out to their customers at a phenomenally low cost. Most importantly, they are real time and allow a marketer to capture markets live.

It is now the marketer's responsibility to ensure that the content generated through social media is constantly updated so as to keep the buzz alive. Social Media allow you to listen to what is being said about your brand, manage your brand through "Online Reputation Management and Tracking" and measure certain important aspects of your brand.

Proper strategising can lead to customers turning into marketers for your brand but at the same time one negative opinion can multiply and cause a serious blow to the brand's image.

If effectively utilized, Social Media empower companies as well as people to have a two way flow of communication facilitating an openness which can go a long way in building the trust of the consumer. Once this trust is established and the brand starts resonating with the consumer's needs, we can say that Social Media have achieved their objectives.

This book also highlights Social Media implementation plans and the important aspects to be considered while integrating social media in your company's marketing strategies.

For any Social Media plan to be implemented the first step is to learn about the various Social Media tools and identify the business opportunities which can tap their potential. Consequently, one can choose and map various Social Media tools with the business activities and relevant content strategies. Finally, Social Media's effectiveness can be measured through pre-defined measurement metrics and then improvised accordingly.

To conclude, Social Media can be very crucial to the extension of your business, as they allow sharing of knowledge and insights, developing business processes, and enable distributed business teams to work together closely to complete predefined tasks.

Some of the case studies highlighted in this book on initiatives like "Save the Tiger" by Aircel, "Garden of Love" by Cadbury, Indianfantasyleague.com for IPL and examples of Coke, HP, etc stand testimony to the influence of Social Media on consumers.

Yet, the main objective of social media should be to engage and interact with the Internet users and at no point of time should companies try and control their behaviour. They should also have the potential to expand and converge with other media so that they advance with technology.

References

1. Bernoff, Jeff, and Charlene Li. Groundswell: Winning in a World Transformed by Social Technologies. Boston, MA: Harvard Business School Press, 2008.
2. Brogan, Chris, and Julien Smith. Trust Agents: Using the Web to Build Influence, Improve Reputation, and Earn Trust. Hoboken, NJ: John Wiley & Sons, 2009.
3. Fox, Vanessa. Marketing in the Age of Google: Your Online Strategy IS Your Business Strategy. New York, NY: Wiley, 2010.
4. Gardner, Susannah, and Shane Birley. Blogging for Dummies. New York, NY: For Dummies, 2008.
5. Godin, Seth. Purple Cow: Transform Your Business by Being Remarkable. New York, NY: Portfolio, 2003.
6. Godin, Seth. Tribes: We Need You to Lead Us. New York, NY: Portfolio, 2008.
7. Goodstein, Anastasia. Totally Wired: What Teens and Tweens Are Really Doing Online. New York, NY: Saint Martin's Griffin, 2007.
8. Israel, Shel. Twitterville: How Businesses Can Thrive in the New Global Neighborhoods. New York, NY: Portfolio, 2009.
9. Kaushik, Avinash. Web Analytics: An Hour a Day. Indianapolis IN: Sybex, 2007.
10. Levine, Rick, and Christopher Locke, Doc Searls, and David Weinberger. The Cluetrain Manifesto: The End of Business as Usual. Cambridge, MA: Basic Books, 2000. Find the book online at http:// www.cluetrain.com/book/.
11. Shirky, Clay. Here Comes Everybody: The Power of Organizing Without Organizations. New York, NY: Penguin Group, 2008.
12. Solis, Brian. Putting the Public Back in Public Relations: How Social Media Is Reinventing the Aging Business of PR. Upper Saddle River, NJ: FT Press, 2009.
13. Weinberger, David. Everything Is Miscellaneous: The Power of the New Digital Disorder. New York, NY: Times Books, 2007.
14. The Gilbane Group, 2008, Collaboration and Social Media-2008, Research Report. [Online] Available at:

    http://www.octopz.com/media/files/Gilbane-Social-Computing-Report-Summary.pdf
15. iPressroom, Eric Schwartzman ,2009, Essential Online Public Relations and Marketing Skills, 2009 Digital Readiness Report [online] Available at:

    http://www.ipressroom.com/pr/corporate/document/ipr_2009_Digital_Readiness_final.pdf
16. Michael. A. Stelzner, 2009, Social Media Marketing Industry Report, How Marketers Are Using Social Media to Grow Their Businesses, Social Media Examiner. [online] Available at: http://marketingwhitepapers.s3.amazonaws.com/smss09/SocialMediaMarketingIndustryReport.pdf

17. TACTİCA, Kevin Glasier, 2009, The Conversation An İntroduction to Social Media [online] Available at:

http://www.slideshare.net/tactica_inc/the-conversation-an-introduction-to-social-media-presentation

18. PWC, 2010, How consumer conversation will transform business [online] Available at:

http://www.pwc.com/gx/en/technology-media-convergence/consumer-conversation-will-transform-business/

19. Sally Falkow, 2009, Social Media Strategy, Expansion Plus, İnc. [online] Available at:

http://www.scribd.com/doc/24682691/Expansion-Plus-Social-Media-Strategies

20. Antony Mayfield, 2008, What İs Social Media?, iCrossing, [online] Available at:

http://www.icrossing.co.uk/fileadmin/uploads/eBooks/What_is_Social_Media_iCrossing_ebook.pdf

21. Brian Solis, 2008, The Essential Guide To Social Media, P.R 2.0 [online] Available at:

http://www.scribd.com/doc/3283966/The-Essential-Guide-to-Social-Media

22. Amber Naslund, 2009,The social media starter kit, altitudebranding [online] Available at:

http://altitudebranding.com/wp_content/uploads/2009/02/SocialMediaStarterKit-Tools.pdf

23. David merman scott, 2008, The Viral Marketing, How Word Of Mouse Spreads Your İdeas For Free, [online] Available at:

http://www.davidmeermanscott.com/documents/Viral_Marketing.pdf

24. Eric Karjaluoto, 2008, A Primer in Social Media, smashlab. [online] Available at:

http://www.smashlab.com/files/primer_in_social_media.pdf

25. Eastman Kodak Company, 2009, Social Media Tips, [online] Available at:

http://www.kodak.com/US/images/en/corp/aboutKodak/onlineToday/Kodak_SocialMediaTips_Aug14.pdf

26. Donald K. Wright, Michelle D. Hinson, 2008, How Blogs and Social Media are Changing Public Relations and the Way it is practiced, [online] Available at:

http://www.prsa.org/SearchResults/views/How_Blogs_and_Social_Media_are_Changing_Public_Rel

27. Rob Williams, 2009, Getting Started with Social Media, [online] Available at:

http://orangejack.com/media/getting_started_with_social_media.pdf

Social Media References

1. http://www.open2media.org/what-is-social-media/the-main-types-of-social-media/
2. http://www.socialbrite.org/sharing-center/glossary/
3. http://www.scribd.com/doc/15011/What-is-Social-Media-Spannerworks-2006
4. http://www.slideshare.net/hasan_99/social-medias-influence-in-purchase-decision
5. http://blissfullydomestic.com/2008/20-reasons-small-businesses-should-use-social-media
6. http://thenorthdakotan.wordpress.com/2009/07/24/20-reasons-your-small-business-should-use-social-media/
7. http://www.acognita.com/index.php/blog/C6/
8. http://www.slideshare.net/kmlaughl/social-networking-ppt
9. http://blog.okcupid.com/index.php/2010/01/20/the-4-big-myths-of-profile-pictures/
10. http://www.articulate.com/rapid-elearning/myth-4-since-anybody-can-now-build-training-i-am-going-to-lose-my-job/
11. http://www.socialwebanalytics.com/The_Social_Web_Analytics_eBook_2008.pdf
12. http://www.markevanstech.com/2009/02/13/the-five-myths-of-social-media/
13. http://www.whatsnextblog.com/archives/2009/02/my_article_in_businessweek_debunking_six_social_media_myths/
14. http://www.danonit.com/blog/2010/04/09/six-free-social-media-tools-to-try-for-yourself
15. http://www.socialmention.com/
16. http://www.honeytechblog.com/top-10-social-media-tracking-and-analytics-tools/
17. http://blog.postrank.com/
18. http://www.techvibes.com/blog/digital-media-people-to-watch-in-ontario-in-2010
19. http://www.web-strategist.com/blog/2008/04/25/companies-that-track-discussions-in-forums-and-communities/
20. http://www.web-strategist.com/blog/category/social-media-measurement/
21. http://www.aboutus.org/BoardTracker.com
22. http://www.socialmediagroup.com/social-media-rfp-template/
23. http://socialmediagroup.com/2010/01/11/social-media-rfp-ask-the-right-questions-find-the-right-partner/
24. http://tc.eserver.org/37025/Social Media